CREATIVE COMPANIES

THE STORY OF TWITTER

SARA GILBERT

JAICO PUBLISHING HOUSE
Ahmedabad Bangalore Chennai
Delhi Hyderabad Kolkata Mumbai

Published by Jaico Publishing House
A-2 Jash Chambers, 7-A Sir Phirozshah Mehta Road
Fort, Mumbai - 400 001
jaicopub@jaicobooks.com
www.jaicobooks.com

Published in arrangement with
The Creative Company
123 South Broad Street, Mankato, MN 56001, USA

To be sold only in India, Bangladesh, Bhutan,
Pakistan, Nepal, Sri Lanka and the Maldives.

Design by Zeno Design, Production by Chelsey Luther
Art Direction by Christine Vanderbeek

Photographs by Alamy (IanDagnall Computing, Art Kowalsky, The NYC collection, David Robertson, Tom K Photo), Corbis (MARIO ANZUONI/Reuters, NOAH BERGER/Reuters, David Brabyn, JOHN GRESS/Reuters, Kim Kulish, ADREES LATIF/Reuters, KIMBERLY WHITE/Reuters), Dreamstime (Pressureua), Flickr (jack dorsey), Getty Images (The Asahi Shimbun, Simon Dawson/Bloomberg, Kevin Mazur/WireImage), Newscom (SHADISHD173/AFP/Getty Images, Soeren Stache/dpa/picture-alliance), Shutterstock (Edyta Pawlowska, Andrew Zarivny), SuperStock (Radius)

THE STORY OF TWITTER
ISBN 978-81-8495-770-9

First Jaico Impression: 2015
Seventh Jaico Impression: 2025

Page design and layout: Special Effects, Mumbai

Printed by
Trinity Academy For Corporate Training Limited, Mumbai

CREATIVE COMPANIES

THE STORY OF TWITTER

In mid-March 2006, a group of young men in San Francisco, California, started brainstorming about a new platform that would allow people to let their friends know what they were up to with short notes. They spent eight days planning and building a website that would host those posts and share them with other users. Finally, at 9:50 P.M. Pacific Standard Time on March 21, 2006, one of those men—Jack Dorsey—posted the first official tweet when an automated message, "just setting up my twttr," went live on the new site. Ten minutes later, Dorsey posted a second message with just 18 quick characters, this one urging the men he had spent the past week working with on the site to join him: "inviting coworkers."

1

The Right Idea

The original plan was to develop a platform for people to listen to podcasts, or recorded audio files, on their MP3 players. Software developer Noah Glass had started a company called Odeo in 2005 to create that technology and, with the financial backing of his friend Evan Williams and others, hired a handful of other developers, web designers, and engineers to help build the system.

The Odeo crew—including Glass, Williams, software engineers Blaine Cook and Christopher "Biz" Stone, and web designer Jack Dorsey—worked long hours in a San Francisco apartment that had been turned into an office space. By July 2005, they had created a platform for podcasting that they thought would be the company's first product. But before their product was ready to be launched, Apple announced that it had built its own podcasting platform and that the platform would be built into every iPod that the company sold.

Apple's announcement, coupled with a realization that even Odeo employees weren't regularly using the technology that they had created to listen to podcasts, forced the company to abruptly change its direction. Late in 2005, Williams challenged the company's 14 employees to come up with new ideas to pursue. They broke into small groups and began holding day-long "hackathons" during which they focused on projects that might lead to the next big thing.

One of the ideas that emerged from those sessions came from Dorsey. He suggested that the company develop a product that would allow people to tell their friends what they were doing at any given time—a concept that he called "status."

It was an idea that Dorsey had been thinking about for several years. As a teenager, he had developed a software that allowed taxi drivers, bike couriers, and package delivery trucks to maintain constant, real-time communication with each other. He thought that same software could be combined with instant-messaging technology to allow friends to share moment-to-moment status updates with each other. He had sketched out his rough idea for the concept, which he called "Stat.Us," on a notepad in 2001, while he was a student at New York University. By the time he joined Odeo in 2006, he still hadn't found the right way to put it into action.

Although Glass admired Dorsey and

Apple's iPod nano has gone through several generations, or models, since its introduction in 2005

considered him to be one of the rising stars in the company, he didn't immediately understand why Dorsey was so excited about the idea of instant status updates. But one rainy night, as he and Dorsey talked while driving home together at the end of a long day, the idea suddenly made sense to him. "I was sitting with Jack and I said, 'Oh, I do see how this could really come together to make something really compelling,'" Glass said. "It all fit together for me."

In February, Glass and Dorsey gathered the Odeo staff and presented the idea of designing a Short Message Service (SMS) system that allowed people to send a text update to one number—40404—that would be simultaneously broadcast to all

Twitter cofounder Jack Dorsey attended New York University but left before earning a degree their friends. Glass had come up with a name for it as well: Twttr, in the same abbreviated style as the photo-sharing website Flickr. He and Dorsey wanted a name that would represent the physical feeling of receiving a text message on a mobile phone, which might vibrate in a person's pocket. Their original idea was "twitch," but they didn't think that would give people the right visual image. They looked in the dictionary and found "twitter" close to "twitch"—and they agreed it was perfect. "The definition was 'a short burst of inconsequential information,' and 'chirps from birds,'" Dorsey said. "And that's exactly what the product was."

The rest of the Odeo team—including Williams—reacted to the idea with much of the same skepticism Glass had originally had. But Williams could tell that Glass was enthusiastic about it and that he had a vision for what it could become. He gave Glass the go-ahead to select a team of Odeo employees to start working on the project. The team labored day and night trying to

Although it has evolved over the years, Twitter has stayed true to its mission of connecting people

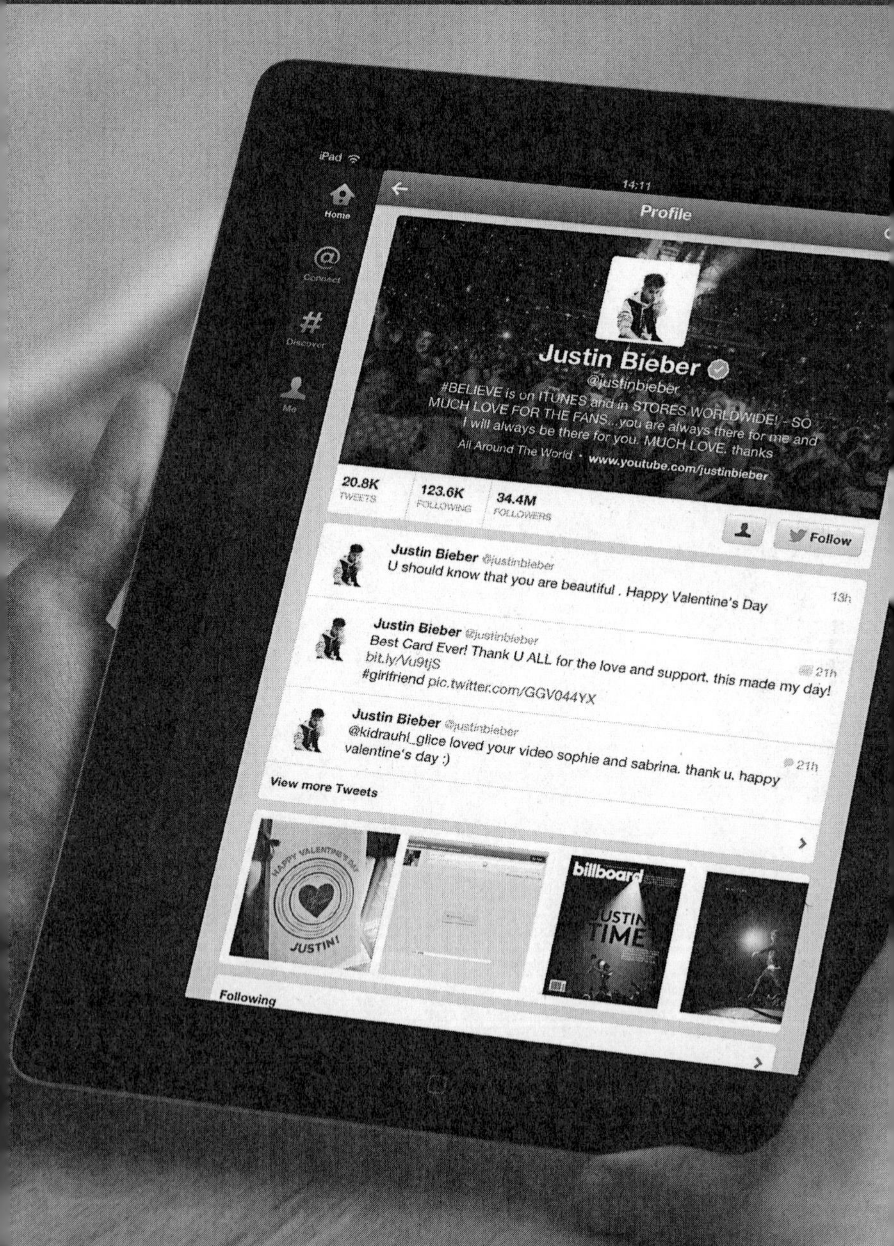
iPad
14:11
Home
Connect
Discover
Me
Profile
Justin Bieber
@justinbieber
#BELIEVE is on ITUNES and in STORES WORLDWIDE! - SO MUCH LOVE FOR THE FANS...you are always there for me and I will always be there for you. MUCH LOVE. thanks
All Around The World • www.youtube.com/justinbieber
20.8K TWEETS
123.6K FOLLOWING
34.4M FOLLOWERS
Follow
Justin Bieber @justinbieber
U should know that you are beautiful . Happy Valentine's Day
13h
Justin Bieber @justinbieber
Best Card Ever! Thank U ALL for the love and support. this made my day! bit.ly/Vu9tjS #girlfriend pic.twitter.com/GGV044YX
21h
Justin Bieber @justinbieber
@kidrauhl_glice loved your video sophie and sabrina. thank u. happy valentine's day :)
21h
View more Tweets
HAPPY VALENTINE'S DAY
JUSTIN!
billboard
JUSTIN TIME
Following

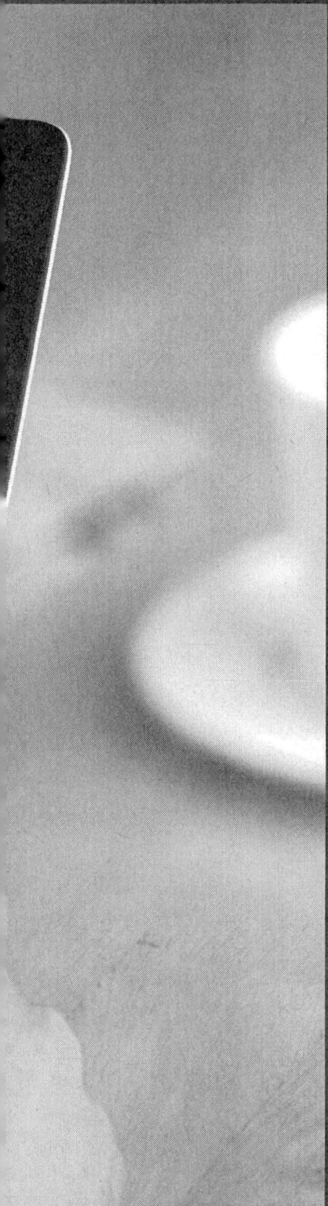

Top Tweeters

With the help of computer algorithms that scan its site, Twitter tallies the top 100 Twitter accounts, in terms of the number of followers, on a daily basis. Many of the same names appear on that list every day, often in the same order. Not surprisingly, most of the top 100 are celebrities. Singers such as Justin Bieber, Lady Gaga, and Rihanna were ranked in the top 10 in mid-2013; so were president Barack Obama and reality TV star Kim Kardashian. Also in the top 100 were a few athletes, including basketball player Shaquille O'Neal, and a couple of news sources, such as cable news channel CNN and The New York Times. Twitter itself even made the list; its Twitter feed had more than 26 million followers in late 2013—fewer than singer Taylor Swift but more than either Nicki Minaj or Bruno Mars.

figure out the programming to make Twttr work. And by mid-March, they got close enough to start using the technology themselves.

What they had was a simple website that allowed users—at the time, just the Odeo employees—to send text messages of 140 characters or fewer about what they were doing. It was on that site that, on March 21, Dorsey posted the first tweet—"just setting up my twttr." His coworkers soon started tweeting, too; one of those coworkers, Dom Sagolla, posted, "Oh, this is going to be addictive."

He was right. By midsummer, the Odeo staff was so obsessed with the service that they racked up hundreds of dollars in phone bills because they had been using the renamed Twitter to send so many messages. Odeo agreed to pay those bills, because it believed Twitter would be worth the investment.

On July 15, 2006, Odeo officially introduced Twitter to the general public. By August, the service had enough users that word of a small earthquake that rattled San Francisco spread quickly through Twitter posts. By fall, thousands of people were using Twitter.

2

Start Tweeting

Despite that promising start, not everyone was convinced that Odeo and Twitter were going to be successful. In September 2006, Evan Williams sent a letter to the investors who had put together $5 million to fund Odeo's launch, suggesting that he buy back their shares in the company.

He was concerned that, although Twitter seemed to show potential, Odeo itself wasn't living up to their earlier expectations and that they might lose money on the company. The investors agreed to his offer and sold all their interest in Odeo—and Twitter—back to him.

That shift in ownership brought with it a few other changes. First, Williams renamed the company Obvious and changed its focus to be an incubator for innovative technological ideas. Then, in a move that surprised most people at Obvious, he fired Noah Glass. His leadership team was now made up of Biz Stone and Jack Dorsey, the latter of whom was known for wearing his hair in a shaggy mop and sporting a tattoo that stretched the length of his forearm. When Dorsey became the company's chief executive officer (CEO), he removed his nose ring so that he could look more like the leader of a successful company.

But success was still slow in coming. Users were certainly joining Twitter, including presidential candidate John Edwards, who used it to announce appearances and speeches to his supporters, and cable news network CNN, which broadcasted news headlines. But they weren't coming aboard in the large numbers that the owners were hoping for. Some saw the medium as mundane and self-centered, and wondered how many people were actually interested in someone else doing their laundry or going to the grocery store.

That all changed in March 2007, when Obvious introduced Twitter to attendees of the South by Southwest music, film, and digital technology conference in Austin, Texas. The company had set up a pair of huge plasma screen televisions near the registration desk in a busy hallway where much of the conference was taking place. The screens ran a stream of tweets people were posting about the event, from interesting panel discussions to upcoming parties or restaurants in the area worth trying.

Suddenly, everyone at the conference was talking about Twitter. Speakers and panelists

TIME listed Biz Stone (pictured) and his Twitter cofounders among 2009's most influential people mentioned it during their programs, and many of the attendees kept track of what their friends were doing through Twitter. People were asking each other if they were on Twitter yet—and many were signing up for the service at the conference. Over the course of the conference, which ran from March 14 to March 18, Twitter usage surged from approximately 20,000 posts a day to more than 60,000.

The buzz generated at South by Southwest helped Twitter tally a total of 400,000 tweets in the first 3 months of 2007. It also led to Williams's decision to spin Twitter off from Obvious, where new technologies were already being pursued, and make it its own company. The only problem was that Twitter still wasn't making

In 2007, Twitter received a boost in users, thanks to South by Southwest festival attendees any money. Users weren't charged any fees, and there was no advertising on the site, either. The company's first focus was on expanding the service to millions of users; finding a revenue stream, Williams said, would come once that goal had been reached: "Hopefully, we'll know how to make money by then," he noted.

In the meantime, however, Twitter's leadership also had to figure out how to make the growing service more reliable for its users. As the number of users grew, Twitter's website suffered numerous outages; in 2007, Twitter-ers received what became known as the "Fail Whale" message, in which a white whale being lifted up by eight orange birds was displayed with the caption, "Too many tweets! Please wait a moment and try again," for a total of 5 days and 23 minutes.

Those outages were affecting important people: In 2008, both Barack Obama and John McCain used Twitter as a tool to reach supporters while campaigning to become the next president of the United States. Celebrities had also started

"Our vision for the company is simple: Twitter brings you closer. You can say something now and broadcast, and everyone around the world sees it immediately."

Dick Costolo,
ceo of Twitter

Designer Yiying Lu originally created the "Fail Whale" as artwork she called "Lifting a Dreamer"

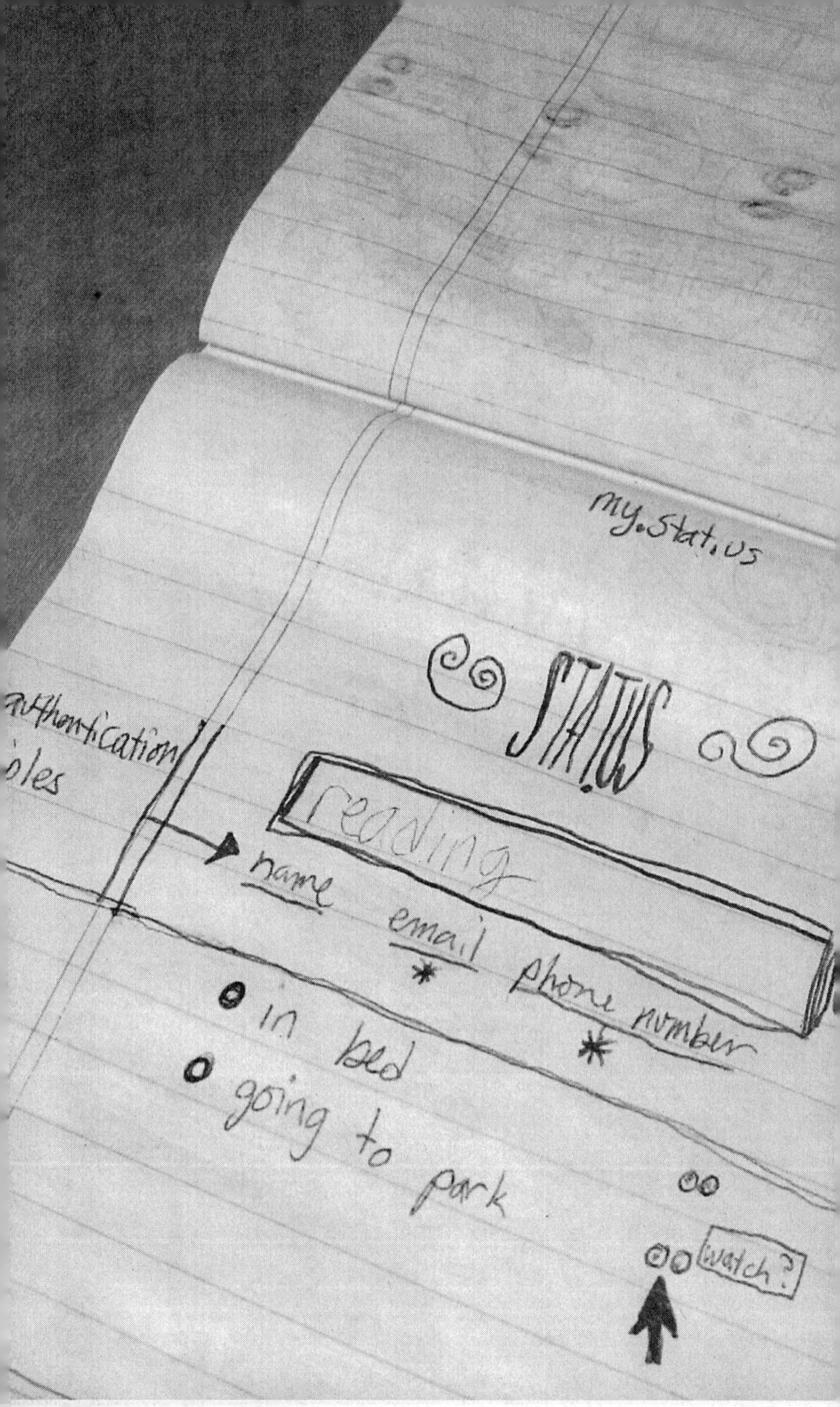
my.Stat.us
STATUS
reading
name
email
phone number
in bed
going to park
watch?

Dorsey's Document

In his office at Twitter, cofounder Jack Dorsey hung a sheet of paper torn from a legal pad on the wall. At the top of that piece of paper was the word "STAT.US", which was the working title for the personal update system that Dorsey had dreamed up while he was a student at New York University in 2000–01. The document laid out the basic plan for how status updates would be posted, with "reading" as the example; it also included two samples of past statuses: "in bed" and "going to park." Next to both of those statuses were a pair of googly eyes, which Dorsey said represented what he called "watching." "You could watch or unwatch someone," he explained. "But [at Twitter], we found a better word—follow or unfollow." Although the final version of Twitter differed slightly from Dorsey's original drawing, the concept remained consistent.

using it; singer Britney Spears was tweeting about her new album, for example, and Wil Wheaton, an actor from *Star Trek: The Next Generation*, was a frequent tweeter. It was also becoming part of popular culture, with mentions on television shows such as *The Big Bang Theory*.

Such attention helped Twitter as it reached out to investors for additional funding. Although more than a 100 million tweets were being posted every quarter in 2008 and registrations had increased by 600 percent over the previous year, the company still had not found a way to make money. Even after Twitter received a $15-million investment from a group of venture capital firms in May 2008, industry experts were concerned that the company's chances of long-term success were limited without a reliable source of revenue.

Twitter's board of directors was so eager to see the company make money that on October 16, 2008, they replaced Dorsey as CEO with Williams; although Dorsey was asked to serve as the chairman of the board, Williams took over the day-to-day operations of the business. "We all think Evan is a better fit to lead the company from a product perspective, an operations perspective, and a business standpoint," said board member and Twitter investor Fred Wilson.

3
All a-Twitter

Twitter's popularity had grown so much that by January 2009, it had become the third-most popular social networking site, behind Facebook and MySpace. It had passed the one-billion tweet mark and was growing at an incredible 1,382 percent rate over the previous year.

It had become so mainstream that the *Associated Press Stylebook*, which provides guidelines to journalists about the acceptable usage of certain words, added several Twitter-based terms—including "to tweet"—and set up its own Twitter account as well. New definitions of "Twitter" as both a noun and a verb were also added to the *Collins English Dictionary*.

Despite Twitter's growing prevalence, especially among adults, the service was still derided by some critics as being irrelevant and boring. In June 2009, talk-show host Conan O'Brien launched a segment called "Twitter Tracker" on *The Tonight Show*. During the segment, he made jokes about celebrity tweets that he considered particularly bland or mundane—actress Jennifer Love Hewitt tweeting about how beautiful the weather was, for example, or actor Ashton Kutcher's tweet about going to the grocery store. Later that summer, an analysis of Twitter by an independent firm separated its content into six different categories; the largest, with 40 percent of all tweets, was labeled "pointless babble."

But the tweets being posted in Iran that June were far from pointless. When Mahmoud Ahmadinejad claimed that he had won that country's presidential election, thousands of protesters took to the streets of the Iranian capital of Tehran as well as other cities in Iran. At first, they communicated with each other, and with the rest of the world, by sending text messages. But when the government blocked cell phone service, cut off the satellite feeds of foreign news agencies covering the event, and censored the content of local newspapers, protesters turned to Twitter instead.

Twitter, which had planned to temporarily shut down its website for routine maintenance on June 16, was flooded with live updates from Iran, eventually reaching 220,000 posts per hour. It was one of the only ways that news of the uprising was reaching the international community, and keeping it running was critical to the U.S. State

In 2009, actor Ashton Kutcher became the first Twitter user to attract 1 and then 2 million followers

Department, which was monitoring the situation as well. The State Department sent an e-mail to Twitter, asking that the scheduled maintenance be postponed. "It appears that Twitter is playing an important role at a crucial time in Iran," the e-mail said. "Could you keep it going?"

Twitter complied with that request and became one of the most consistent sources of news throughout the revolution; major news outlets, including CNN and the British Broadcasting Corporation (BBC), used tweets from Iran in addition to videos uploaded to the YouTube website to piece together reports about the uprising.

Twitter's role in keeping the world apprised of the situation in Iran added credibility to its service.

When Iran's government censored communications in 2009, citizens shared photos through Twitter

But the high volume of tweets also stressed the company's servers. Things got even worse on June 25, 2009, when American pop singer Michael Jackson died. Users were posting updates about his death at a rate of 100,000 tweets per hour, which caused Twitter's server to crash and the service to run slowly for a brief time.

By October 2009, Twitter had tallied more than 5 billion total tweets. But it still hadn't made its first dollar of profit. Rumors had started circu-lating that a plan was in place for Twitter to find revenue and that the company anticipated bringing in almost $4.5 million by the end of the year. But no details about how the company intended to make that much money were available.

Despite those predictions, the year ended without any revenue. Twitter claimed approx-imately 18 million users worldwide—a huge number compared with the 6 million registered uses at the end of 2008 but still just a fraction of the more than 250 million Facebook users. And

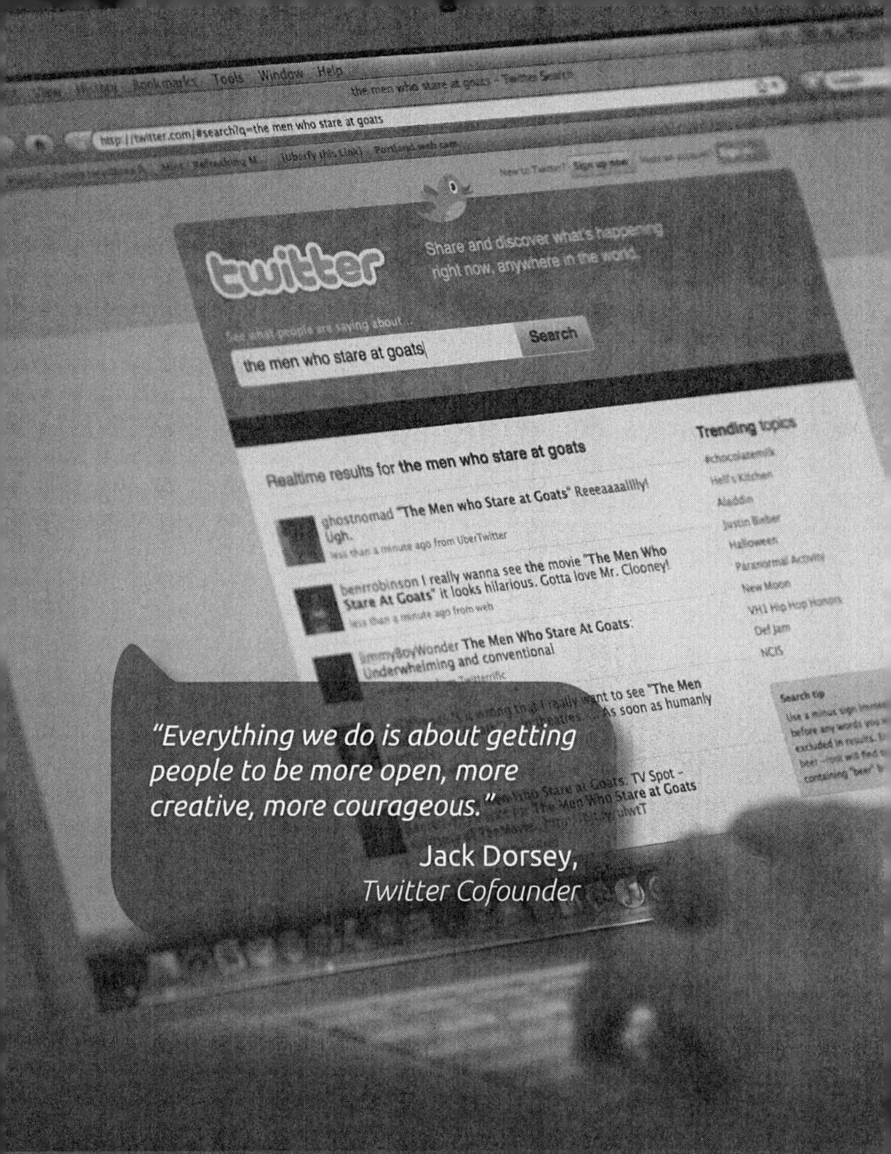

"Everything we do is about getting people to be more open, more creative, more courageous."

Jack Dorsey,
Twitter Cofounder

"Trending topics" lets users view the trending, or most popular, subjects that others are discussing

For the Birds

In its first six years, Twitter used three different logos. The first was just its name, written in blue, bubbly lowercase letters; the second, which was introduced in September 2010, again used the name, all in bubbly lowercase letters, but this time colored black—and with a small blue bird at the end of the word. The logo that Twitter unveiled in 2012 showed a similar bright blue bird that appeared to be chirping happily as it flew, with no words at all. According to Doug Bowman, the creative director who oversaw the design of the logo, the bird is designed after a mountain bluebird and is intended to represent "freedom, hope, and limitless possibility." It also connects to one of the definitions of the word twitter—chirps from birds. "Bird chirps sound meaningless to us," cofounder Jack Dorsey said. "But meaning is applied to other birds. The same is true of Twitter."

unlike Facebook, which was able to report that almost half of its users checked the site at least once a day, Twitter had only a 40 percent retention rate, which meant that 60 percent of the people who registered for Twitter accounts didn't remain active users. Concerns about the company's long-term viability surfaced again.

Early in 2010, as Twitter usage exceeded 50 million tweets each day, the company finally announced its strategy for making money. Companies could purchase "promoted tweets" that would appear in certain search results on Twitter's website—an advertising model quite similar to Google's AdWords, which had helped the popular search engine turn a profit. When the program was introduced in April 2010, several companies were already eager to participate, including Sony Pictures, Best Buy, Red Bull, and Starbucks.

As the ads rolled out, Twitter usage continued to grow. Three times during the month of June, it set, and then broke, records for the most tweets per second. On June 14, users posted 2,940 tweets per second during a World Cup soccer game between Japan and Cameroon; 3 days later, 3,085 tweets per second were posted following the Los Angeles Lakers' victory over the Boston Celtics in the National Basketball Association (NBA) playoffs. Later in the month, that record was broken as well, when 3,283 tweets per second were sent during another World Cup match—this one between Japan and Denmark. By the end of the summer, Twitter had more users than MySpace.

4

Focused on Growth

In October 2010, Evan Williams stepped down as the CEO of Twitter. He had done what the board asked him to do when they put him in that position by implementing an advertising program that would bring in more than $45 million in revenue by the end of the year. Although that wasn't enough for the company to turn its first profit, it gave investors, confidence that the company at least had the potential to make money.

Williams became a member of Twitter's board; Dick Costolo, who had been Twitter's chief operating officer and a crucial leader when it came to establishing a revenue stream, took over for him.

Costolo's focus remained on revenue during the first part of 2011. Some industry watchers were predicting that Twitter would make at least $150 million in 2011—more than triple what it had made the previous year. The company was attracting large advertisers with deep pockets, including credit card company American Express, Coca-Cola, and computer maker Dell. But to make that much money, the company would need to continue increasing the number of people using the service so that advertisers would be convinced that their ads were having an impact.

As Twitter executives were worrying about how the company would make that much money, other companies were taking note of its growing value. In February, the *Wall Street Journal*, a newspaper that covers business dealings, reported that both Facebook and Google had expressed an interest in purchasing Twitter for as much as $10 billion—an enormous sum for a company that had still not turned a profit. Although Twitter didn't seriously entertain the idea of selling at that time, the reports of those offers helped Twitter prove its worth to potential advertisers.

In March, as Twitter was celebrating its fifth birthday, Costolo recruited a familiar face to help him expand the company's base: Jack Dorsey. After leaving Twitter in 2008, Dorsey had started a new company called Square, which allowed people to use mobile phones to process credit card payments. Its offices were just a few blocks away from Twitter headquarters in San Francisco; Dorsey, who planned to continue as the CEO of Square as well, could walk between the two offices. Fittingly, he announced his return to the company he helped start with a tweet: "Today I'm thrilled to get back to work at @Twitter leading product as Executive Chairman. And yes: leading @Square forevermore as CEO."

Twitter CEO Dick Costolo, a former stand-up comedian, gained a reputation for humorous tweets

His return was seen by many people both inside and outside the company as a positive step and an effort to return to Twitter's innovative roots. In his new role as the executive chairman, Dorsey would be in charge of product development. His job, he said, was to listen to what users wanted and to help encourage growth by creating just that—while also making sure that efforts to increase advertising revenue didn't take away from the core product. "Getting Jack back kind of completes the picture of getting us focused on the next phase of the company's growth," said Peter Fenton, a member of Twitter's board.

With Dorsey taking the leadership role, Twitter quickly introduced

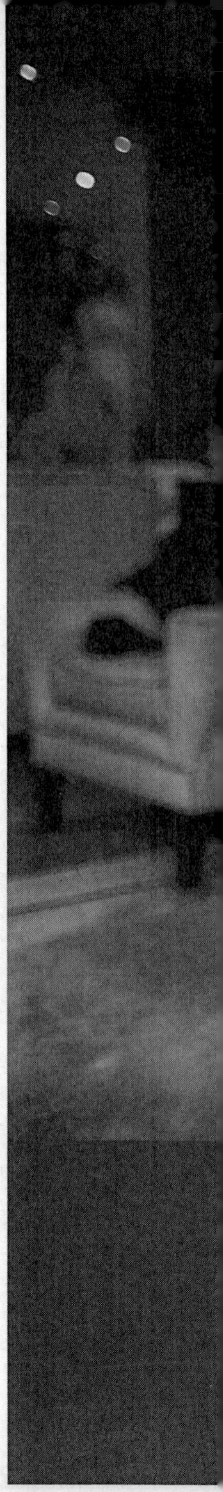

Jack Dorsey's stakes in both Twitter and Square made him a billionaire by age 35

a number of changes, from a new, sleeker version of its website homepage to an improved search tool that made it easier to find followers. In May, it also unveiled a "Follow" button that could be placed on websites by both individuals and companies to encourage others to follow their Twitter feed. In June, additional changes made it possible for users to place photos and videos in their tweets.

By the end of June 2011, more than 200 million tweets were being posted every day—the equivalent of publishing a 10-million-page book daily. Although many of those tweets were still based on daily activities such as shopping, exercising, and eating, throughout the years, Twitter had become

"I get all my news from Twitter."

Piers Morgan,
Talk-show Host on CNN

When a devastating tsunami hit Japan in 2011, Twitter was a source for up-to-the-minute news

Where are they Now?

Twitter was officially founded by four men: Noah Glass, Jack Dorsey, Christopher "Biz" Stone, and Evan Williams. Only one of them—Dorsey—was still connected to the company as of 2013. He gave up his day-to-day role at the company in 2008 and went on to start another technology-based business, Square, which allows mobile phones to process credit card payments. Dorsey returned to Twitter in 2011 as the executive chairman, a position that allowed him to oversee the company's product development. Stone was still at Twitter when Dorsey returned in March 2011, but he resigned in June to rejoin Williams, who had stepped down as Twitter's CEO, at Obvious—the company from which Twitter spun off in 2006. They planned to use Obvious as a laboratory for new ideas and to "create products that matter," Williams said. Glass, who was fired in 2006, returned to San Francisco after a long absence, where he was working on developing green technologies.

more and more valuable as a communication tool for major events as well.

Early in 2011, Twitter had been used extensively by Egyptian citizens demanding that their president resign as part of what became known as the Arab Spring—a period of time during which countries led by dictators and corrupt politicians rose up to bring about a change in leadership. In March, Twitter users in Japan had used the service to spread the news of the devastating earthquake and tsunami there. And in May, when Al-Qaeda leader Osama bin Laden was killed, more than 5,000 tweets were sent per second as the news of his death was confirmed.

Twitter was growing so fast—it hit 100 million active users in September—that it opened two new offices. The first, in Dublin, Ireland, gave the company an international presence. The second was located on Madison Avenue in New York City—a strategic site for the company to be. Not only did New York have more users than any other city in the world at that time, but it was also home to many of the advertisers that Twitter was eager to build relationships with so that it could reach its revenue goals sooner. Dorsey and New York City mayor Michael Bloomberg were both at the office for Twitter's grand opening in October, and they both tweeted the news of its opening from the site.

5
Tweeting to the Top

Not long after revealing its new digs in New York, Twitter unveiled a new look for its virtual home as well. The redesigned version of Twitter.com that was launched on December 9, 2011, certainly looked different; its components were rearranged on the page, and an enhanced navigation bar was placed prominently at the top. But the changes went beyond just the appearance of the page. They were also meant to make Twitter easier to use—especially for new users.

"It's not just a visual redesign but a conceptual redesign to make Twitter more accessible to the next billion users," said Satya Patel, a senior executive at Twitter.

But Twitter wanted to do more than attract another billion users. It also wanted to reel in more advertisers so that it could make more money. At the end of 2011, the company had reached revenues of almost $140 million and was hoping to increase that figure to almost $260 million in 2012. Although some rumors that Twitter might sell shares and become a public company had surfaced, it was still privately owned—which meant that it didn't have to publicly report its profits. But with 900 employees and new offices opening in Detroit, Michigan; Tokyo, Japan; and other locations around the world, the cost of keeping Twitter in business seemed to be growing as fast as the revenue it was bringing in.

So as its number of users, and the number of daily tweets, continued to increase, Twitter worked on creating more options for advertisers—including having promoted tweets directly on mobile applications of the service. It also set its sights on establishing a more international pool of advertisers. Although less than half of all Twitter users were based in the U.S., at least 90 percent of its ads in 2011 were generated by American companies. And, with an eye on the U.S. presidential election scheduled for November, Twitter also began hinting that it might accept paid political advertising in the fall. "We have figured out the business," Costolo confirmed. "The advertising model is working."

Although other technology startups had seen greater monetary success faster—Google had reached the $1-billion mark in only five years, and Facebook crossed that threshold after six—Twitter's growth had impressed many of the same analysts who had been concerned about the company's future just a few years earlier. As Twitter turned six on March 21, Dorsey tweeted a happy-birthday wish to the company: "From 1 tweet to over 1 billion every 3 days," he wrote.

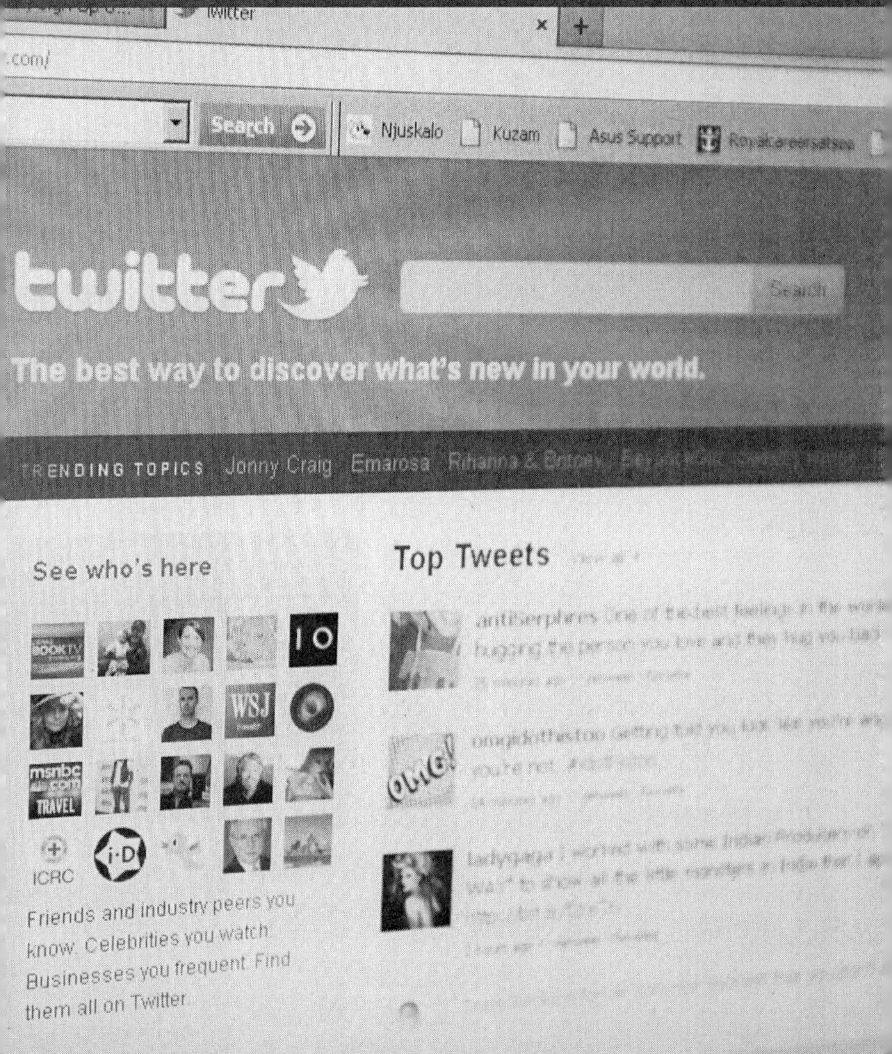

In 2007, Twitter users began using hashtags, or # symbols, to mark keywords of their posts

"I'm so proud of our users and our team."

Just three months later, he was tweeting from a new home. Twitter moved its headquarters to a historic building in San Francisco's Central Market neighborhood—a run-down area of town that the city had committed to revitalize. The 11-story building it moved into had been empty for the past 5 years, and Twitter's decision to lease the first 3 floors of it was seen as a first step in cleaning up the neighborhood and stimulating economic growth in the area. The city of San Francisco was so eager to have the company occupy the building that it had provided a lucrative tax break to make it possible.

On the June day that Twitter's San Francisco-based employees

""When you have a mass of people updating about a particular thing, you're exposing a trend: This is happening right now in this location or on this topic. It gives you an immediacy and relevancy for what people are talking about right now." "

Jack Dorsey,
Twitter Cofounder

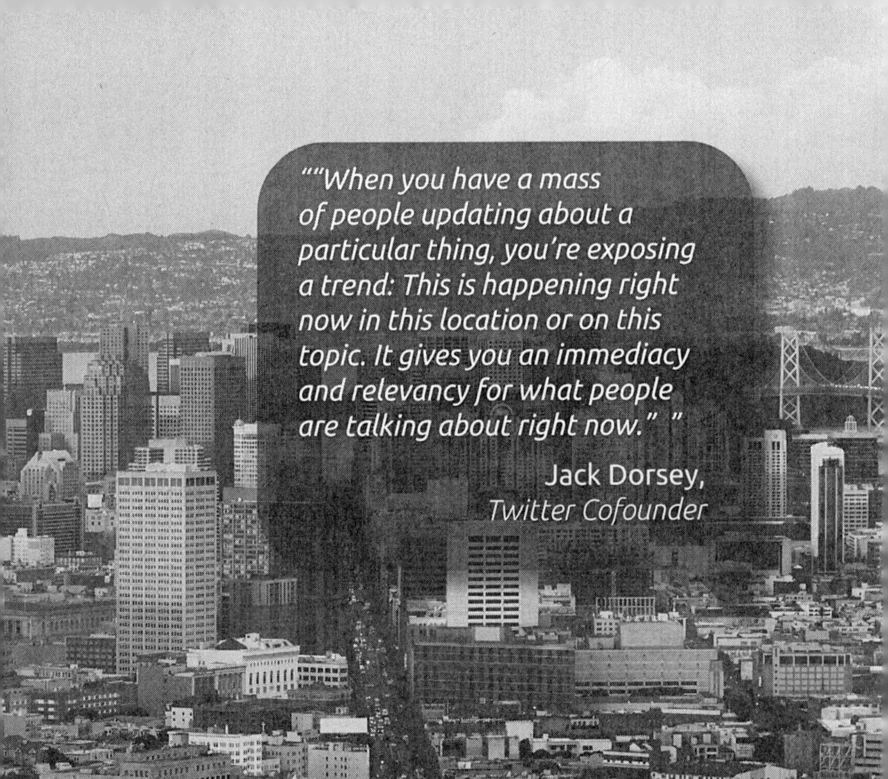

Twitter's hometown of San Francisco is luring ever more tech-related businesses to its crowded streets moved into the new space, the company hosted a barbecue on the rooftop deck. Several of the employees tweeted pictures of the event and of the office space, including the skee ball games in the arcade, the yoga studio, and the rooftop garden. Fittingly, the building was decorated with artwork featuring birds—including the happy little blue bird that had been adopted as the company's official logo earlier in the month.

Those little birds had a lot to chirp about during the company's first few months in the new space. Twitter was growing at a faster rate than rival social networking site Facebook and had become more widely used in Japan than Facebook. Thanks to advertising revenue as well as outside funding

Twitter expanded its staff and office spaces worldwide, setting the stage for future innovation

Who Tweets?

In 2013, the Pew Research Center, which conducts polls about issues, attitudes, and trends, released the results of its annual survey about Internet use—including Twitter and other social media websites—by the American public. They found that in 2012, 16 percent of adults who used the Internet used Twitter, second only to Facebook, which 67 percent used. The survey revealed that Twitter is most appealing to adults between the ages of 18 and 29, African Americans, and people who live in urban areas. Women were slightly more likely than men to use Twitter. According to similar research by Ignite Social Media, not even half of all Twitter users in 2012 lived in the U.S. Of the cities worldwide with the largest bases of Twitter users, only two—New York and Los Angeles—were in the U.S. Caracas, Venezuela, had the most users, followed by Jakarta, Indonesia, and Sao Paulo, Brazil.

from investors (including Prince Alwaleed bin Talal of Saudi Arabia, who put $300 million into the company at the end of 2011), Twitter had "truckloads of money in the bank," Costolo said.

When 2012 ended with revenues of more than $350 million, some analysts speculated that the company could reach $1 billion within two years. In November 2013, Twitter decided to go public by selling shares of ownership in the growing company. But even as Twitter focused on increasing revenue, it also kept concentrating on upgrading the services it provided to users and to improving its value as a communications tool for the masses, from incorporating video capabilities to simplifying user interactions. "We're just focused on building the best platform and making sure it's up and stable," Dorsey said.

Although billions of tweets have been posted since Dorsey announced that he was setting up the first Twitter account in 2006, the company remains committed to the simplicity of that first post. Twitter has grown in many ways since then, but its focus on providing a means for people to update others about their activities has never changed. As users continue tweeting into the future, it likely never will.

Glossary

algorithms a process or set of rules to be followed in specific operations, especially by a computer

board of directors a group of people in charge of making decisions for a publicly owned company

censored having been removed from print or blacked out after review by official sources

couriers messengers who transport goods or documents

economic having to do with the system of producing, distributing, and consuming of goods within a society

engineers people who design, build, and maintain systems for specific uses

incubator in business, a place where resources and support are provided to allow new ideas to develop

investment the purchase of shares of companies or other organizations in exchange for ownership in that company or organization

lease to rent property or land from its owner

platform the base from which new computer programs and applications can be built and operated

profit the amount of money that a business keeps after subtracting expenses from income

quarter one of four three-month intervals that together comprise the financial year

revenue the money earned by a company; another word for income

search engine a website whose primary function is locating information available on the Internet

servers the main computers in a network, or group of linked computers, on which shared programs and files are stored

shares the equal parts a company may be divided into; shareholders each hold a certain number of shares, or a percentage, of the company

social networking linking a group of people in an online setting by common ties, such as friendship, employment, or other affiliations

software written programs or

rules that control a computer's operations

startups companies that are in the early stages of operation

tax break a concession or advantage related to taxes allowed by the government

uprising an act of resistance or rebellion; a revolt

urban relating to the characteristics of a city

venture capital funds made available to small businesses that are starting out but show great potential for growth

Selected Bibliography

Carlson, Nicholas. "The Real History of Twitter." Business Insider, April 13, 2011.

Mashable. "Twitter Rewind: Big Highlights from 2012 to 2006." http://mashable.com/2012/03/21/history-of-twitter
-timeline/.

New York Times. "Twitter News." Business Day. http://topics
.nytimes.com/top/news/business/companies/twitter/index
.html.

O'Reilly, Tim, and Sarah Milstean. The Twitter Book. Sebastopol, Calif.: O'Reilly Media, 2011.

Sarno, David. "Twitter Creator Jack Dorsey Illuminates the Site's Founding Document." Los Angeles Times, February 18, 2009.

Twitaholic. "Top Twitter User Rankings and Stats." http://twitaholic.com/.

Index

A
advertisers 43, 44, 52, 55, 56
Apple Inc. 7

B
Bowman, Doug 39
British Broadcasting Corporation (BBC) 34

C
Caracas, Venezuela 63
celebrity users 15, 24, 28, 31
CNN 15, 20, 34, 49
Cook, Blaine 7
Costolo, Dick 25, 43, 44, 45, 56, 64
critics 31

D
Detroit, Michigan 55
Dorsey, Jack 5, 7, 8, 10, 11, 12, 16, 19, 28, 34, 37, 39, 44, 47, 51, 53, 56, 64, 68

F
Facebook 30, 36, 44, 56, 60, 63
Fenton, Peter 46

G
Glass, Noah 6, 7, 8, 10, 12, 19, 51
Google 40, 44, 56

I
Ignite Social Media 63
investors 118, 19, 24, 42, 64

J
Japan 40, 41, 49, 52, 55, 60

M
Morgan, Piers 49
MySpace 30, 41

N
New York City 52, 53

O
O'Brien, Conan 31
Obvious 14, 16, 37
Odeo 6, 7, 8, 10, 12, 16, 18, 19

P
Patel, Satya 55
Pew Research Center 63

S
Sagolla, Dom 16
San Francisco, California 5, 7, 16, 44, 51, 58, 60
Short Message Service (SMS) 10
South by Southwest conference 20, 22
Square 44, 47, 51
Stat.Us 8, 27
Stone, Christopher "Biz" 7, 19, 21, 51

T
text messages 8, 10, 24
tweets 5, 15, 16, 18, 20, 22, 24, 28, 30, 31, 32, 34, 36, 40, 41, 44, 45, 48, 52, 53, 54, 55, 56,58, 60, 63, 64
- character limits 16
- content analysis 31, 32
- promoted 40, 56

Twitter
- as communication tool 35, 52, 64
- employment 7, 12, 16, 55, 60

first tweet 5, 16
headquarters 44, 58
known as Twttr 5, 12, 16
logo 39, 60
mainstream adoption 31
naming of 12, 16
outages 24
profits 36, 40, 42, 44, 55
public launch 16
retention rates 40
revenue 24, 28, 36, 42, 43, 46, 53, 55 60, 64
spinoff from Obvious 22
top accounts 15
usage statistics 16, 19, 22 24, 31 36, 40, 41, 52, 55, 56, 63
website 5, 10, 21, 24, 32, 44, 48

W

Wall Street Journal 43
Williams, Evan 6, 7, 12, 18, 19, 22, 24, 28, 42, 43, 51
Wilson, Fred 29

Y

YouTube 34

JAICO PUBLISHING HOUSE

Elevate Your Life. Transform Your World.

ESTABLISHED IN 1946, Jaico Publishing House is home to world-transforming authors such as Sri Sri Paramahansa Yogananda, Osho, the Dalai Lama, Sri Sri Ravi Shankar, Sadhguru, Robin Sharma, Deepak Chopra, Jack Canfield, Eknath Easwaran, Devdutt Pattanaik, Khushwant Singh, John Maxwell, Brian Tracy, and Stephen Hawking.

Our late founder Mr. Jaman Shah first established Jaico as a book distribution company. Sensing that independence was around the corner, he aptly named his company Jaico ('Jai' means victory in Hindi). In order to service the significant demand for affordable books in a developing nation, Mr. Shah initiated Jaico's own publications. Jaico was India's first publisher of paperback books in the English language.

While self-help, religion and philosophy, mind/body/spirit, and business titles form the cornerstone of our non-fiction list, we publish an exciting range of travel, current affairs, biography, and popular science books as well. Our renewed focus on popular fiction is evident in our new titles by a host of fresh young talent from India and abroad. Jaico's recently established translations division translates selected English content into nine regional languages.

Jaico distributes its own titles. With its headquarters in Mumbai, Jaico has branches in Ahmedabad, Bangalore, Chennai, Delhi, Hyderabad, and Kolkata.

SINCE 1946